AF430139

Brave, Not Perfect

Brave, Not Perfect

Embracing Vulnerability to Create a Life of Courage

B. Vincent

QuantumQuill Press

CONTENTS

Copyright © 2024 by B. Vincent

All rights reserved. No part of this book may be reproduced in any manner whatsoever without written permission except in the case of brief quotations embodied in critical articles and reviews.

First Printing, 2024

Chapter 1: The Myth of Perfection

Describing Faultlessness

In our high level world, the possibility of faultlessness immerses each piece of our lives. From the photos of immaculate greatness put across online diversion to the tireless mission for impeccability in our work and associations, perfection is apparently a conclusive goal. Be that as it may, what definitively is perfection?

Faultlessness is generally speaking portrayed by social standards and individual convictions that immediate what is viewed as great or awesome. These rules can vary comprehensively dependent upon culture, adolescence, and individual experiences. Nevertheless, the secret message go on as in the past: faultlessness is something to be accomplished, something to have a go at regardless.

We are attacked regularly with pictures and messages that development this idea of faultlessness. We see carefully decorated models and huge names gracing the fronts of magazines, their ideal appearance setting an inaccessible standard for greatness. We hear records of compelling business visionaries who appear to effortlessly investigate the business world, their achievements delineating perfect accomplishment. Regardless of these endless standards, it's no huge astonishment that so many of us feel lacking and questionable.

Nevertheless, envision a situation where we were to challenge this idea of perfection. Envision a situation where we were to reevaluate being perfect. Envision a situation in which, as opposed to making a pass at an inaccessible ideal, we were to embrace our imperfections and recognize our uniqueness.

In the parts that follow, we will explore the dangers of seeking after faultlessness and the liberating power of embracing imperfection. We will sort out some way to perceive the mission for significance and the journey for faultlessness, and we will find how embracing imperfection can incite a presence of intensity, validity, and fulfillment. So let us set out on this journey together, as we loosen up the legend of perfection and embrace the radiance of our flawed selves.

The Dangers of Chasing after Faultlessness

In our enduring mission for perfection, we much of the time disregard to see the expense it takes on our flourishing. We drive ourselves to fulfill unimaginable rules, relinquishing our mental and significant prosperity at the same time. The dangers of chasing after faultlessness are far reaching, impacting each piece of our lives.

One of the most tricky dangers of seeking after perfection is the expense it takes on our profound health. The reliable strain to be faultless can incite anxiety, demoralization, and other mental wellbeing issues. We become consumed by self-vulnerability and dread about frustration, ceaselessly attempting to fulfill unthinkable rules that fundamental undermine our character worth.

Seeking after perfection in like manner adversely influences our genuine prosperity. The strain and pressure related with gaining ground toward perfection can show up in genuine secondary effects like headaches, lack of sleep, and stomach related issues. We dismiss our bodies in mission for our goals, pushing ourselves to the brink of exhaustion and burnout.

In any case, perhaps the most serious gamble of seeking after faultlessness is the expense it takes on our associations. Exactly when we center around perfection over affiliation, we disregard to truly attract with individuals around us. We become occupied with our own imperfections and frailties, unsuitable to totally show up for people we care about. Our associations persevere accordingly, letting us feeling isolated and be.

This moment is the best opportunity to see the dangers of chasing after faultlessness and recuperate our lives from its grip. We ought to sort out some way to zero in on our flourishing over irrational standards of faultlessness, embracing our imperfections and complimenting our uniqueness. Truly around then could we anytime really continue with a presence of mental backbone, validness, and fulfillment.

Revealing the Legend

As we adventure further into the examination of faultlessness, it becomes essential to unravel the legend that includes it. We ought to perceive the journey for significance and the persisting mission for a far off great. This present time is the best opportunity to strip back the layers of social suppositions and individual convictions to reveal reality under the outside of perfection.

The mission for significance is a good endeavor laid out being developed and self-improvement. It is connected to trying to be the best version of ourselves, stretching past our boundaries, and showing up at our most extreme limit. Significance perceives that perfection is a trickiness, seeing that there is reliably space for improvement and improvement.

Of course, the journey for perfection is a constant mission for flawlessness laid out in fear and shortcoming. It is empowered by the conviction that our worth is joined to our ability to fulfill limitless rules, inciting a consistent example of self-examination and connection. Hairsplitting prevents us from getting our fulfillment and keeps us from getting our validity, leaving us feeling vacant and unfulfilled.

By uncovering the legend of faultlessness, we free ourselves from its smothering handle. We begin to see that blemish isn't something to be feared anyway something to be embraced. We sort out some way to recognize our imperfections and eccentricities as a show of our human-ity, seeing that our blemishes make us truly beautiful.

This present time is the best opportunity to give up the legend of perfection and embrace the chaotic, imperfect reality of life. This present time is the best opportunity to let ourselves out of the heaviness of crazy suspicions and live, heroically, and sincerely. Truly around then could we anytime really exemplify the core of fearlessness and step into the fruition of what our personality is planned to be.

Embracing Deformity

Pursuing backbone and validity, maybe of the most exceptional step we can take is to embrace imperfection. It is through embracing our deformities that we begin to foster the intensity to live truly and genu-inely. Regardless, what's the importance here to embrace abandon?

Embracing flaw is connected to giving up the ought to be impeccable and enduring ourselves definitively as we are. It is connected to seeing that faultlessness is an inaccessible ideal and that our worth isn't por-trayed by our ability to satisfy incomprehensible rules. Right when we embrace imperfection, we free ourselves from the abuse of assessment and self-judgment, allowing ourselves to be feeble and genuine.

In any case, embracing blemish is for the most part troublesome. It anticipates that we should face our most significant sensations of fear and frailties, to surrender the covers we wear to hide our flaws. It antici-pates that we should embrace shortcoming and to accept that we really merit love and affirmation correspondingly as we are.

Regardless, the honors of embracing imperfection are enormous. Exactly when we embrace blemish, we let loose ourselves to a vast expanse of credibility and improvement. We become more grounded despite torment, more accommodating towards ourselves as well as others, and more strong as we continued looking for validity.

Embracing flaw isn't connected to consenting to average quality or inconsiderateness. It is connected to seeing that perfection is a tricki-ness and that veritable greatness lies in our flaws and imperfections. It is connected to embracing the chaotic, imperfect reality of life and finding the psychological courage to live strikingly and authentically in spite of it.

So let us embrace imperfection with extraordinary friendship and open hearts, understanding that it is through our defects that we track down our most authentic selves. Permit us to compliment our flaws and unconventionalities as a show of our humanity and let us embrace the trip of self-revelation with mettle, sympathy, and excellence.

2 |

Chapter 2: The Power of Vulnerability

Grasping Weakness

Weakness is frequently misconstrued and dreaded, yet it holds enormous power in our excursion towards self-improvement and credible living. To genuinely saddle this power, we should initially comprehend what weakness is and why it is fundamental in our lives.

At its center, weakness is the readiness to appear and be seen, in any event, when there are no certifications of progress or acknowledgment. It is the mental fortitude to speak the truth about our viewpoints, sentiments, and encounters, in any event, when they cause us to feel uncovered and awkward. Weakness isn't shortcoming; it is strength in its most flawless structure.

At the point when we embrace weakness, we free ourselves up to the full scope of human experience. We permit ourselves to feel profoundly, to adore earnestly, and to seek after our fantasies with enduring assurance. It is through weakness that we interface with others on a more profound level and fashion significant connections based on trust and realness.

Nonetheless, weakness can likewise be overwhelming, particularly in a world that frequently esteems strength and emotionlessness over transparency and weakness. We dread judgment, dismissal, and disparagement, so we take cover behind veils and walls, hesitant to allow others to see the genuine us.

In any case, actually, weakness is the origin of mental fortitude, imagination, and association. It is through weakness that we view the mental fortitude as ourselves completely and genuinely. It is through weakness that we tap into our innovativeness and release our actual potential. What's more, it is through weakness that we fabricate profound and significant associations with others, making a feeling of having a place and local area.

So let us embrace weakness with great affection and open hearts, realizing that it is through our weakness that we track down our actual strength and fortitude. Allow us to embrace the untidy, flawed truth of life and allowed us to appear, be seen, and live sincerely, each weak move toward turn.

Dissipating Confusions

In our general public, weakness is much of the time apparent as a shortcoming, something to be kept away from no matter what. We are educated to conceal our weaknesses, to act courageously and imagine that all is great, in any event, when it's not. In any case, imagine a scenario where we were to challenge these confusions and perceive the truth about weakness: a wellspring of solidarity and credibility.

Scattering the misinterpretations encompassing weakness is fundamental assuming we are to embrace its power in our lives completely. It expects us to scrutinize the stories that let us know weakness is inseparable from shortcoming and to reevaluate weakness as a brave demonstration of self-articulation.

In opposition to prevalent thinking, weakness is certainly not an indication of shortcoming yet rather an indication of solidarity. It takes fortitude to appear and be seen, to permit ourselves to be weak in a world that frequently esteems flawlessness and safety. At the point when we embrace weakness, we show our readiness to be legitimate and consistent with ourselves, in any event, when it's awkward.

Additionally, weakness isn't tied in with broadcasting our filthy clothing or looking for consideration; it's tied in with speaking the truth about our encounters and feelings. It's tied in with recognizing our apprehensions and uncertainties and permitting ourselves to be defectively human. At the point when we embrace weakness, we make space for certified association and closeness, as others are attracted to our validness and weakness.

Scattering the misinterpretations encompassing weakness is a freeing act that liberates us from the shackles of dread and disgrace. It permits us to appear completely in our lives, to embrace our blemishes, and to associate with others in a profound and significant manner. So let us challenge the thought that weakness will be shortcoming and on second thought embrace it as a wellspring of boldness, genuineness, and association.

Developing Self-Empathy

At the core of weakness lies the urgent act of self-sympathy. It is through self-empathy that we can sustain and recuperate our internal identities, embracing weakness as a way to self-acknowledgment and love.

Developing self-sympathy starts with recognizing and tolerating our weaknesses without judgment or analysis. Rather than criticizing ourselves for our apparent deficiencies, we offer ourselves benevolence and understanding, perceiving that we are human and meriting affection and empathy.

Self-sympathy permits us to embrace our defects with tenderness and compassion, instead of unforgiving self-analysis. It is the counteractant to disgrace and self-question, offering us a shelter of graciousness and acknowledgment even with our most profound feelings of dread and instabilities.

Yet, developing self-sympathy is generally difficult, particularly in a culture that frequently esteems confidence and sturdiness over weakness and empathy. We might oppose being delicate with ourselves, seeing it as an indication of shortcoming instead of solidarity. In any case, it is definitively in our snapshots of weakness that we want self-empathy the most.

Rehearsing self-empathy is a groundbreaking excursion that requires tolerance, diligence, and mindfulness. It includes figuring out how to treat ourselves with the very thoughtfulness and understanding that we would propose to a dear companion, perceiving that we genuinely deserve love and empathy similarly as we are.

At the point when we develop self-sympathy, we make an underpinning of inward strength and versatility that permits us to explore life's difficulties with effortlessness and boldness. We become more tolerating of ourselves as well as other people, cultivating further associations and connections based on trust and sympathy.

So let us develop self-sympathy with expectation and reason, realizing that it is through consideration and acknowledgment that we track down the boldness to embrace weakness and live genuinely. Allow us to treat ourselves with the very empathy and understanding that we would propose to other people, perceiving that self-sympathy is the way to opening the force of weakness in our lives.

Building Valid Associations

Fundamental to the force of weakness is its capacity to cultivate veritable associations with others, established in legitimacy and trust. By embracing weakness, we make the space for profound and significant connections to thrive, based on an underpinning of transparency and genuineness.

Building legitimate associations starts with being willing to appear and be seen, in any event, when it's awkward. It expects us to relinquish our veils and walls and to permit ourselves to be open to other people, sharing our actual considerations, sentiments, and encounters unafraid of judgment or dismissal.

At the point when we embrace weakness in our connections, we welcome others to do likewise. We make a place of refuge where everybody goes ahead and act naturally, realizing that they will be acknowledged and cherished genuinely. Along these lines, weakness turns into the money of association, permitting us to produce securities that are profound, significant, and enduring.

However, building credible associations additionally expects us to be available and sympathetic with others. It includes genuinely paying attention to other people, approving their encounters, and offering backing and understanding without judgment or exhortation. At the point when we approach our associations with sympathy and empathy, we establish a climate where weakness can flourish, encouraging closeness and association.

Nonetheless, building true associations is generally difficult, particularly in a world that frequently esteems superficial cooperations over profound, significant connections. It expects us to be powerless and to face challenges, realizing that the awards of genuine association far offset the dangers of dismissal or disloyalty.

Eventually, building bona fide associations is a groundbreaking excursion that enhances our lives in endless ways. It permits us to encounter the delight of genuine having a place, realizing that we are acknowledged and cherished for who we really are. It extends our associations with others, encouraging a feeling of local area and backing that supports us through life's high points and low points.

So let us embrace weakness as the way to building valid associations with others, realizing that it is through our ability to be seen and acknowledged that we track down the genuine excellence and lavishness of human association. Give us develop weakness access our associations with expectation and reason, realizing that it is the establishment whereupon genuine associations are fabricated.

Chapter 3: Overcoming Fear of Failure

The Feeling of dread toward Disappointment

The feeling of dread toward disappointment is an unavoidable power that prowls in the shadows of our brains, prepared to undermine our endeavors and dreams every step of the way. It is brought into the world from a profoundly instilled conviction that disappointment is something to be stayed away from no matter what, an indication of deficiency and dishonor. Yet, what precisely is the anxiety toward disappointment, and how can it appear in our lives?

At its center, the feeling of dread toward disappointment is established in an anxiety toward judgment and dismissal. We stress over what others will suppose assuming we miss the mark regarding assumptions, expecting that disappointment will lessen our value according to other people. This dread drives us to leave nothing to chance, to adhere to the natural and agreeable as opposed to wandering into the obscure where disappointment prowls.

In any case, the anxiety toward disappointment isn't just about outside judgment; it is likewise about how we see ourselves. We incorporate the conviction that disappointment mirrors our inborn imperfections and deficiencies, prompting sensations of disgrace and self-question. We become caught in a pattern of compulsiveness, continually endeavoring to demonstrate our value through our accomplishments and victories.

Be that as it may, the anxiety toward disappointment is definitely not an intrinsic quality but instead a learned reaction to our encounters and climate. It is molded by our childhood, our way of life, and our previous encounters of achievement and disappointment. In any case, similarly as it is educated, it can likewise be untaught, supplanted by another outlook that sees disappointment not as a danger but rather as a chance for development and learning.

In the parts that follow, we will investigate systems for conquering the feeling of dread toward disappointment and embracing another attitude established in strength and boldness. We will figure out how to reexamine disappointment as a characteristic piece of the excursion towards progress, and we will find the force of persistence despite misfortune. So let us stand up to the apprehension about disappointment head-on, realizing that it is exclusively by overcoming our feelings of trepidation that we can genuinely develop and flourish.

Reexamining Disappointment

In our general public, disappointment is in many cases seen as a wellspring of disgrace and deficiency, a red letter that marks us as contemptible and uncouth. Be that as it may, imagine a scenario in which we were to challenge this restricted perspective on disappointment and recognize the truth about it: a characteristic and unavoidable piece of the human experience.

Reexamining disappointment includes moving our viewpoint to see difficulties not as indications of inadequacy or shamefulness, but rather as any open doors for development and learning. It expects us to relinquish the conviction that disappointment is something to be kept away from no matter what and on second thought embrace it as an important instructor on the excursion towards progress.

In any case, rethinking disappointment is generally difficult, particularly in a culture that frequently esteems flawlessness and accomplishment regardless of anything else. We might expect that recognizing our disappointments will lessen our value according to other people, driving us to conceal our errors and deficiencies as opposed to face them head-on.

In any case, truly disappointment isn't something contrary to progress; it is a venturing stone on the way to progress. Each fruitful individual has encountered disappointment en route; it is the manner by which they answer disappointment that separates them. Rather than allowing inability to overcome them, they use it as fuel to drive them forward, gaining from their missteps and becoming more grounded and stronger simultaneously.

Reevaluating disappointment expects us to develop a development outlook, one that considers difficulties to be potential open doors and misfortunes as venturing stones to progress. It includes relinquishing our connection to results and embracing the excursion of development and self-disclosure. At the point when we view disappointment from this perspective, we enable ourselves to face challenges, attempt new things, and seek after our fantasies with mental fortitude and assurance.

So let us reexamine disappointment not as a wellspring of disgrace or deficiency, but rather as a significant chance for development and learning. Allow us to embrace our disappointments with lowliness and elegance, realizing that it is through our errors that we become more grounded, savvier, and stronger. Furthermore, let us recall that disappointment isn't the stopping point however simply a diversion on the way to progress.

Embracing Versatility

Even with disappointment, versatility is our most prominent resource. It is the capacity to return quickly more grounded still up in the air than any other time in recent memory, to continue on despite misfortune and arise victorious. Yet, what precisely is strength, and how might we develop it in our own lives?

Versatility isn't tied in with staying away from disappointment or difficulty; it is about how we answer them. It is the eagerness to stand up to our difficulties head-on, to adjust and fill despite affliction, and to rise up out of troublesome times with newly discovered strength and insight.

Be that as it may, developing strength is generally difficult, particularly when we are confronted with mishaps and dissatisfactions. We might feel overpowered by our conditions, enticed to surrender or withdraw into despair. Notwithstanding, it is definitively at these times that strength turns out to be generally urgent.

To develop flexibility, we should initially recognize and acknowledge our disappointments and mishaps without judgment or self-analysis. We should permit ourselves to feel our feelings completely, perceiving that it is alright to encounter trouble, disillusionment, and dissatisfaction. By recognizing our sentiments, we can start to handle them and push ahead with lucidity and reason.

Then, we should zero in on developing our internal fortitude and flexibility through taking care of oneself and self-empathy. This includes dealing with our physical, profound, and mental prosperity, and supporting ourselves with graciousness and understanding. By focusing on taking care of oneself, we can recharge our energy saves and develop the versatility expected to explore life's difficulties with beauty and mental fortitude.

At last, we should develop an outlook of diligence and assurance, declining to be crushed by disappointment or difficulties. Rather than harping on our slip-ups, we should zero in on the illustrations they train us and use them as fuel to drive us forward. By embracing a development mentality and review disappointment as a chance for learning and development, we can develop the flexibility expected to conquer any deterrent that holds us up.

Eventually, versatility isn't tied in with keeping away from disappointment or difficulty, yet about how we answer them. It is tied in with embracing our difficulties with fortitude and assurance, realizing that it is through affliction that we develop and flourish. So let us develop flexibility in our own lives, realizing that it is the way to defeating any snag and accomplishing our most prominent dreams.

Observing Little Triumphs

In the midst of the quest for our amazing desires, disregarding the meaning of little triumphs en route is simple. Nonetheless, these apparently minor victories assume a critical part in our excursion of self-awareness and improvement, filling in as achievements of progress and wellsprings of inspiration.

Celebrating little triumphs includes moving our concentration from the ultimate objective to the steady advances we take towards it. It's tied in with recognizing and regarding the headway we make, regardless of how little, and perceiving the work and assurance it took to accomplish them.

In a culture that frequently praises unexpected phenomenon and great accomplishments, it's memorable's critical that genuine advancement is based upon a groundwork of steady exertion and determination. Every little triumph we celebrate is a demonstration of our flexibility and assurance, demonstrating that even the littlest forward moving steps are critical on the way to progress.

Yet, celebrating little triumphs isn't just about perceiving our own accomplishments; it's likewise about developing a mentality of appreciation and appreciation for the actual excursion. It's tied in with tracking down euphoria and satisfaction during the time spent development and self-disclosure, as opposed to hanging tight for a far off objective to give us joy.

Besides, celebrating little triumphs permits us to develop a feeling of force and energy in our lives. It's tied in with gathering positive speed by recognizing our advancement and involving it as fuel to push us forward towards our objectives. By commending our victories, we construct trust in our capacities and reinforce our purpose to keep pushing towards our fantasies.

Eventually, celebrating little triumphs is a strong practice that enables us to embrace the excursion of self-improvement and improvement with delight and appreciation. It's tied in with tracking down significance and satisfaction during the time spent turning out to be, as opposed to focusing on some far off objective of progress. So let us praise our little triumphs with satisfaction and appreciation, realizing that each step in the right direction carries us nearer to the existence we imagine for ourselves.

Chapter 4: Stepping Out of Your Comfort Zone

The Safe place Trap

The safe place is an enchanting spot, offering commonality and security in a world loaded up with vulnerability and chance. It's where we have a good sense of security and in charge, safeguarded from the distress and difficulties that accompany venturing into the unexplored world. Yet, while the safe place might feel like a shelter from the mayhem of life, additionally a snare keeps us stale and keeps us from arriving at our maximum capacity.

The safe place trap is treacherous on the grounds that it calms us into lack of concern, persuading us that remaining inside its limits is the most secure and most reasonable choice. We become so acclimated with the natural schedules and propensities that we neglect to see the open doors for development and experience that lie just past our usual range of familiarity.

Yet, actually, development and achievement lie beyond our usual range of familiarity. It is simply by venturing into the obscure, by facing challenges and embracing uneasiness, that we can extend our points of view and understand our actual potential. At the point when we stay inside our usual range of familiarity, we restrict ourselves to an existence of unremarkableness and botched open doors.

Besides, the safe place trap smothers our self-improvement as well as impedes our expert turn of events. In the present quickly impacting world, achievement frequently expects us to adjust and advance, to step beyond our usual ranges of familiarity and embrace new difficulties with mental fortitude and flexibility. The people who grip to the well-being of their usual ranges of familiarity risk being abandoned in an always advancing scene.

In the sections that follow, we will investigate methodologies for breaking liberated from the safe place trap and embracing the distress and vulnerability that accompany venturing into the unexplored world. We will figure out how to recognize the restricting convictions and fears that keep us caught inside our usual ranges of familiarity and foster the mental fortitude and certainty to go ahead with reasonable courses of action in quest for our objectives.

So let us see the truth about the safe place trap: a hindrance to our development and potential. Allow us to step strikingly into the obscure, realizing that it is simply by embracing inconvenience and vulnerability that we can genuinely flourish and carry on with an existence of satisfaction and reason.

Distinguishing Restricting Convictions

Installed inside the safe place are a plenty of restricting convictions that build up our hesitance to step past its limits. These convictions, frequently profoundly instilled and subliminal, go about as imperceptible obstructions, keeping us bound to a thin scope of conceivable outcomes and keeping us from arriving at our maximum capacity.

Distinguishing these restricting convictions is the most important move towards breaking liberated from the safe place trap. It expects us to focus a light on the oblivious considerations and convictions that keep us down, carrying them into the front of our mindfulness so we can challenge and defeat them.

Normal restricting convictions that keep us caught inside our usual ranges of familiarity incorporate apprehension about disappointment, feeling of dread toward dismissal, and apprehension about vulnerability.

We might accept that disappointment is an impression of our value, that dismissal is inescapable assuming we step beyond our usual ranges of familiarity, or that vulnerability is something to be stayed away from no matter what.

In any case, these convictions are just deceptions, contortions of reality that keep us caught in examples of dread and aversion. They come from previous encounters and cultural molding, however they don't characterize what our identity is or what we are equipped for accomplishing.

By focusing a light on these restricting convictions, we can start to challenge their legitimacy and supplant them with additional enabling convictions that help our development and achievement. We can develop a mentality of overflow and probability, realizing that disappointment isn't an impression of our value, yet rather a characteristic and inescapable piece of the excursion towards progress.

In the parts that follow, we will investigate procedures for distinguishing and defeating restricting convictions, enabling ourselves to break liberated from the safe place trap and step strikingly into the unexplored world. We will figure out how to develop a mentality of versatility and plausibility, embracing inconvenience as an impetus for development and change.

So let us focus a light on the restricting convictions that keep us down, realizing that it is exclusively by standing up to them head-on that we can break liberated from the limits of our usual ranges of familiarity and understand our actual potential.

Going ahead with Potentially dangerous courses of action

Getting out of our usual ranges of familiarity requires boldness, yet it likewise requests an essential methodology. Proceeding with carefully weighed out courses of action is tied in with exploring the scarcely discernible difference between pushing our limits and guaranteeing our security and prosperity. It includes gauging the possible compensations against the likely outcomes and settling on informed choices in view of cautious thought and evaluation.

One of the vital parts of going ahead with reasonable plans of action is understanding that not all dangers are made equivalent. A few dangers might offer critical potential for development and prize, while others might present pointless risk or mischief. By knowing between the two, we can zero in our energy and assets on those dangers that offer the best potential for positive results.

Additionally, proceeding with carefully thought out plans of action expects us to embrace uneasiness and vulnerability, realizing that development and achievement lie on the opposite side of our feelings of trepidation. It includes venturing into the obscure with fortitude and versatility, confiding in our capacities to explore anything difficulties might emerge en route.

In any case, proceeding with carefully weighed out courses of action isn't about aimlessly pulling out all the stops; it's tied in with relieving expected gambles and boosting our odds of coming out on top. This might include careful exploration and arranging, looking for exhortation from confided in coaches or companions, and having emergency courses of action set up on the off chance that things don't go true to form.

At last, proceeding with reasonable plans of action is tied in with pushing our limits and growing our usual ranges of familiarity in quest for our objectives and dreams. It's tied in with embracing the adventure of experience and the fervor of plausibility, realizing that development and achievement anticipate the people who set out to step strikingly into the unexplored world.

In the parts that follow, we will investigate methodologies for removing reasonable plans of action and venturing from our usual ranges of familiarity with certainty and boldness. We will figure out how to evaluate expected dangers and prizes, foster versatility notwithstanding vulnerability, and develop a mentality of development and probability.

So let us embrace the test of going ahead with potentially dangerous courses of action, realizing that it is through venturing beyond our usual ranges of familiarity that we can genuinely develop and flourish. Allow us to hope against hope enormous and seek after our objectives with strength and assurance, confiding in our capacities to conquer anything that impediments might hinder us.

Embracing Distress

Distress is frequently seen as something to be stayed away from no matter what, a sign that we are wandering beyond our usual ranges of familiarity and into the unexplored world. Nonetheless, uneasiness is likewise a strong impetus for development and change, pushing us past our apparent restrictions and driving us towards our most elevated potential.

Embracing uneasiness is tied in with reevaluating our relationship with distress and vulnerability, remembering them as vital pieces of the excursion towards progress and satisfaction. It includes inclining toward the uneasiness instead of avoiding it, realizing that it is through embracing inconvenience that we can genuinely develop and flourish.

One of the vital parts of embracing distress is developing an outlook of versatility and persistence. It's tied in with perceiving that uneasiness is brief and that we have the strength and flexibility to beat anything difficulties might come our direction. By embracing distress with mental fortitude and assurance, we can change it from an obstruction into a venturing stone on the way to progress.

Besides, embracing inconvenience is tied in with developing a feeling of interest and receptiveness to new encounters. It's tied in with venturing beyond our usual ranges of familiarity and investigating additional opportunities with a receptive outlook and heart. At the point when we embrace distress along these lines, we free ourselves up to a universe of development and probability, permitting us to find gifts and qualities we never realized we had.

Yet, maybe in particular, embracing distress is tied in with confiding in ourselves and our capacities to explore anything difficulties might come our direction. It's tied in with perceiving that distress is a characteristic piece of the human experience and that we are equipped for adapting to the situation and beating anything that deterrents might hold us up.

In the parts that follow, we will investigate systems for embracing uneasiness and venturing strikingly into the unexplored world. We will figure out how to develop strength notwithstanding vulnerability, to incline toward uneasiness with fortitude and assurance, and to confide in our capacities to beat anything that difficulties might come our direction.

So let us embrace uneasiness as a strong impetus for development and change, realizing that it is through venturing beyond our usual ranges of familiarity that we can genuinely arrive at our most elevated potential. Allow us to incline toward inconvenience with mental fortitude and flexibility, realizing that it is through embracing distress that we can genuinely flourish and carry on with an existence of direction and satisfaction.

5 |

Chapter 5: Cultivating Self-Compassion

Figuring out Self-Sympathy

At the center of our capacity to explore life's difficulties with flexibility and elegance lies the idea of self-sympathy. However, time after time, we find it simpler to stretch out consideration and understanding to others than to ourselves. Understanding self-sympathy includes perceiving the significance of treating ourselves with the very warmth and compassion that we would propose to a dear companion in the midst of hardship.

Self-empathy isn't about egocentrism or self indulgence; it's tied in with perceiving our own enduring with thoughtfulness and understanding. It includes recognizing our battles and blemishes without judgment or self-analysis, embracing ourselves with the very unrestricted love and acknowledgment that we would propose to other people.

Research has shown that self-empathy is a strong indicator of versatility, prosperity, and self-improvement. At the point when we develop self-empathy, we become stronger despite affliction, better ready to adapt to pressure and misfortunes, and more roused to seek after our objectives and dreams.

Besides, self-empathy cultivates a more profound feeling of association and having a place, both with ourselves and with others. By perceiving our own mankind and embracing our battles with sympathy, we become more merciful and sympathetic towards others, cultivating further and more significant connections simultaneously.

In any case, developing self-sympathy is generally difficult, particularly in a culture that frequently esteems confidence and strength over weakness and empathy. We might oppose being delicate with ourselves, seeing it as an indication of shortcoming instead of solidarity. In any case, it is unequivocally in our snapshots of weakness that self-empathy turns out to be generally vital.

In the sections that follow, we will investigate procedures for developing self-empathy and coordinating it into our day to day routines. We will figure out how to rehearse self-benevolence, embrace our normal humankind, and develop care for of encouraging more noteworthy self-sympathy and prosperity.

So let us embrace the groundbreaking force of self-sympathy, realizing that it is through treating ourselves with benevolence and understanding that we can genuinely flourish and carry on with an existence of importance and satisfaction.

Rehearsing Self-Thoughtfulness

In the excursion towards self-sympathy, perhaps of the most groundbreaking practice we can take part in is that of self-generosity. This training includes broadening warmth, understanding, and care to ourselves, particularly in snapshots of battle or disappointment.

Rehearsing self-consideration starts with developing a disposition of tenderness and acknowledgment towards ourselves, in any event, when we miss the mark regarding our own assumptions. Rather than censuring ourselves for our missteps or inadequacies, we offer ourselves uplifting statements and backing, treating ourselves with the very delicacy and empathy that we would propose to a friend or family member.

Yet, rehearsing self-benevolence isn't just about the words we share with ourselves; it's likewise about the moves we make to sustain and really focus on ourselves. This might include participating in taking care of oneself exercises that recharge our energy and feed our spirits, like cleaning up, taking a stroll in nature, or investing time with friends and family.

Besides, rehearsing self-generosity includes perceiving our innate worth and deservingness of affection and sympathy, no matter what our accomplishments or disappointments. It's tied in with recognizing that we deserve generosity and care just by ethicalness of being human, with our defects as a whole and flaws.

Nonetheless, rehearsing self-generosity is generally difficult, particularly in a culture that frequently esteems self-analysis and compulsiveness over self-sympathy and acknowledgment. We might oppose being thoughtful to ourselves, seeing it as narcissistic or self centered. Nonetheless, it is unequivocally in snapshots of battle or disappointment that self-graciousness turns out to be generally vital.

In the sections that follow, we will investigate procedures for rehearsing self-generosity and coordinating it into our regular routines. We will figure out how to develop a mentality of self-sympathy, embrace our flaws with beauty and acknowledgment, and indulge ourselves with the benevolence and care that we merit.

So let us practice self-graciousness with goal and reason, realizing that it is through treating ourselves with delicacy and sympathy that we can genuinely flourish and carry on with an existence of significance and satisfaction.

Embracing Normal Humankind

In our individualistic culture, it's not difficult to feel secluded in our battles, accepting that we are the only ones confronting difficulties or encountering torment. Nonetheless, embracing normal mankind includes perceiving that enduring is a general piece of the human experience. We are in good company in our battles; endless others have strolled comparative ways and confronted comparative hindrances.

Embracing normal mankind is tied in with developing a feeling of association and having a place with others, perceiving that our encounters of torment and enduring join us as opposed to isolate us.

It includes relinquishing the deception of flawlessness and recognizing our common weaknesses and blemishes.

At the point when we embrace normal mankind, we develop sympathy and empathy towards ourselves as well as other people. We perceive that it's alright to battle, to commit errors, and to miss the mark concerning our goals. Rather than making a decision about ourselves brutally for our apparent deficiencies, we expand graciousness and understanding, realizing that we are doing all that can be expected in the conditions.

Besides, embracing normal mankind encourages a feeling of fortitude and backing inside our networks. At the point when we recognize and share our battles transparently, we make space for others to do likewise, cultivating a culture of sympathy, empathy, and backing.

Yet, embracing normal humankind is generally difficult, particularly in a culture that frequently esteems independence and confidence over weakness and association. We might expect that recognizing our battles will cause us to seem powerless or inept, driving us to take cover behind veils of solidarity and flawlessness.

Nonetheless, truly embracing normal humankind is a wellspring of solidarity, not shortcoming. It permits us to break liberated from the disengagement of our singular battles and find solace and backing in the information that we are in good company. It enables us to appear really in our connections, realizing that weakness is an indication of boldness, not shortcoming.

In the parts that follow, we will investigate systems for embracing normal mankind and developing a feeling of association and having a place with ourselves as well as other people. We will figure out how to relinquish the deception of flawlessness and embrace our common humankind with empathy and generosity.

So let us embrace normal mankind with open hearts and receptive outlooks, realizing that it is through our common battles that we track down strength, versatility, and association. Allow us to develop sympathy and empathy towards ourselves as well as other people, realizing that we are better off sticking together than going alone, exploring the promising and less promising times of life admirably well.

Developing Care

At the core of self-sympathy lies the act of care, an amazing asset for developing mindfulness and acknowledgment of our viewpoints, feelings, and encounters. Developing care includes fostering the capacity to notice our internal world with interest and non-critical mindfulness, permitting us to answer ourselves with thoughtfulness and sympathy.

Care includes carrying our undivided focus to the current second, without judgment or connection to our viewpoints and sentiments. It's tied in with tuning into our inward encounters with transparency and interest, permitting whatever emerges to be recognized and acknowledged without obstruction.

By developing care, we form more noteworthy understanding into our viewpoints and feelings, permitting us to answer them with more noteworthy lucidity and insight. We become less receptive to our inward encounters, ready to explore them with composure and empathy.

Besides, care encourages a more noteworthy feeling of association and presence in our lives. At the point when we are completely present in every second, we are better ready to associate with ourselves as well as other people, cultivating further and more significant connections all the while.

Yet, developing care is generally difficult, particularly in a world loaded up with interruptions and requests. We might end up got up to speed in our viewpoints and feelings, unfit to break liberated from the pattern of rumination and stress. In any case, with training and persistence, we can figure out how to develop care in our day to day routines, permitting it to turn into a wellspring of solidarity and flexibility.

In the parts that follow, we will investigate methodologies for developing care and coordinating it into our regular routines. We will figure out how to develop present-second mindfulness, form more noteworthy understanding into our inward encounters, and answer ourselves with benevolence and sympathy.

So let us embrace the act of care with open hearts and receptive outlooks, realizing that it is through developing mindfulness and acknowledgment of our internal encounters that we can genuinely flourish and carry on with an existence of significance and satisfaction.

Chapter 6: Building Resilience

Figuring out Versatility

Strength is something beyond returning from difficulty; it's tied in with flourishing despite difficulties and arising more grounded not entirely settled than any other time. Understanding flexibility includes digging into the multifaceted snare of variables that add to our capacity to endure and conquer life's hardships.

At its center, versatility is the ability to adjust and fill despite affliction. It's tied in with tackling our internal strength and assets to explore through troublesome times with mental fortitude and versatility, as opposed to surrendering to despondency or rout. Versatility isn't tied in with being immune to stress or difficulty; it's about how we answer affliction and misfortune and return from mishaps with strength and assurance.

However, flexibility is certainly not a decent characteristic; an expertise can be developed and created over the long haul. It includes building a tool stash of techniques and assets to assist us with adapting to pressure, defeat snags, and keep up with profound prosperity despite misfortune. By understanding the variables that add to flexibility, we can find proactive ways to fortify our versatility and flourish despite life's difficulties.

Research has shown that flexibility is impacted by various variables, including our connections, outlook, methods for dealing with hardship or stress, and social encouraging group of people. By developing these variables, we can fabricate our strength and better endure the unavoidable highs and lows of life.

Besides, understanding versatility includes perceiving that misfortunes and disappointments are an unavoidable piece of the human experience. As opposed to review them as indications of shortcoming or deficiency, we can consider them to be potential open doors for development and learning. By embracing misfortune with boldness and flexibility, we can rise up out of troublesome times more grounded, savvier, and stronger than any time in recent memory.

In the parts that follow, we will investigate procedures for building versatility and developing the internal strength and assets expected to flourish despite affliction. We will figure out how to develop versatility, foster survival methods, and encourage social encouraging groups of people to support our flexibility and explore life's difficulties with mental fortitude and assurance.

So let us set out on this excursion of understanding strength with open hearts and receptive outlooks, realizing that it is through developing versatility that we can genuinely flourish and carry on with an existence of importance and satisfaction.

Figuring out Versatility

Strength isn't simply the capacity to quickly return from misfortune; a powerful cycle includes adjusting and flourishing notwithstanding difficulties. To comprehend versatility is to perceive its diverse nature and its significant effect on our capacity to explore life's highs and lows with elegance and assurance.

At its center, flexibility is tied in with tackling our internal strength and assets to conquer misfortune and arise more grounded and stronger than previously. It's turning around misfortunes and difficulties with mental fortitude and strength, instead of surrendering to sadness or rout.

Be that as it may, versatility isn't just about individual strength; it's likewise about the help and assets accessible to us in our networks and conditions. It's tied in with perceiving the significance of social associations, strong connections, and admittance to assets in building versatility and beating misfortune.

Besides, versatility is certainly not a decent characteristic; an expertise can be developed and created over the long haul. By building our versatility gets past training and experience, we can turn out to be better prepared to explore life's difficulties with certainty and strength.

In the parts that follow, we will investigate techniques for building versatility and beating affliction. We will figure out how to saddle our internal strength and assets, develop steady connections, and foster survival methods to explore life's difficulties with flexibility and beauty.

So let us embrace the force of strength, realizing that it is through confronting difficulties with mental fortitude and assurance that we can genuinely flourish and carry on with an existence of importance and satisfaction.

Point 2: Developing Versatility

Life is intrinsically capricious, loaded up with exciting bends in the road that challenge our feeling of solidness and security. Developing versatility is tied in with fostering the capacity to explore these vulnerabilities with adaptability and elegance, embracing change as a chance for development and change.

Versatility includes being available to new encounters and points of view, able to step beyond our usual ranges of familiarity and embrace the unexplored world. About perceiving change is unavoidable and figuring out how to adjust to new conditions with flexibility and inventiveness.

Yet, developing versatility is generally difficult, particularly when confronted with startling difficulties or disturbances. We might feel impervious to change, gripping to natural schedules and propensities as a wellspring of solace and security. Notwithstanding, it is definitively at these times of inconvenience and vulnerability that versatility turns out to be generally significant.

To develop flexibility, we should initially foster an outlook of receptiveness and interest, embracing change as a characteristic and unavoidable piece of the human experience. We should relinquish our connection to results and embrace the excursion of development and self-revelation, realizing that change is much of the time the impetus for individual change.

Besides, developing flexibility includes fostering the abilities and systems expected to explore change with versatility and elegance. This might include rehearsing care to remain present at the time, creating critical thinking abilities to beat deterrents, and looking for help from others when required.

In the parts that follow, we will investigate methodologies for developing flexibility and embracing change with strength and elegance. We will figure out how to explore life's vulnerabilities with boldness and assurance, realizing that it is through embracing change that we can genuinely flourish and carry on with an existence of importance and satisfaction.

Creating Ways of dealing with hardship or stress

Life is loaded up with difficulties, both of all shapes and sizes, and creating viable survival methods is fundamental for exploring these deterrents with versatility and beauty. Methods for dealing with especially difficult times are the devices and strategies we use to oversee pressure, defeat affliction, and keep up with close to home prosperity despite life's highs and lows.

One vital part of creating survival techniques is perceiving that not all stressors are inside our control. While we will most likely be unable to control outside conditions, we have some control over how we answer them. By creating viable survival methods, we can fabricate versatility and flexibility, permitting us to explore life's difficulties effortlessly and certainty.

Viable survival techniques come in many structures, and what works for one individual may not work for another. Certain individuals find comfort in proactive tasks like activity or yoga, while others might lean toward care rehearses like reflection or profound breathing activities. All things considered, others might find solace in imaginative outlets like composition, painting, or playing music.

No matter what the particular survival methods we pick, the key is to find procedures that impact us actually and integrate them into our day to day routines. Consistency is vital; the more we practice our survival methods, the more successful they become at assisting us with overseeing pressure and keep up with close to home prosperity.

Besides, creating survival methods includes building a tool stash of strategies that we can draw upon in the midst of hardship. Similarly as a woodworker has various instruments for various errands, so too would it be a good idea for us we have a scope of survival methods available to us. This might include trying different things with various procedures and approaches until we find what turns out best for us.

In the sections that follow, we will investigate different survival methods and strategies for overseeing pressure, beating snags, and keeping up with close to home prosperity. We will figure out how to fabricate a tool kit of survival methods that we can draw upon in the midst of hardship, enabling us to explore life's difficulties with flexibility and elegance.

So let us embrace the act of creating survival methods with open hearts and receptive outlooks, realizing that it is through building flexibility and versatility that we can genuinely flourish despite misfortune.

Encouraging Social Help

In the midst of misfortune, perhaps of the most impressive asset we have is the help of others. Encouraging social help includes major areas of strength for developing with companions, family, and local area individuals to give an organization of help during troublesome times.

Social help comes in many structures, from daily reassurance, where companions and friends and family offer a listening ear and uplifting statements, to instrumental help, where they give viable help and assets to assist us with adapting to difficulties. Whether it's a source of genuine sympathy, some assistance, or basically a consoling presence, social help can have a massive effect in our capacity to quickly return from mishaps and conquer difficulty.

Besides, social help gives a feeling of having a place and association, which is fundamental for keeping up with close to home prosperity and versatility. At the point when we feel associated with others, we are better ready to face life's hardships with effortlessness and strength, realizing that we are in good company in our battles.

Yet, cultivating social help isn't just about getting help from others; it's additionally about offering backing to people around us in their critical crossroads. By sustaining solid connections and being there for others when they need us, we make a culture of common help and correspondence, where everybody feels esteemed and upheld.

In the sections that follow, we will investigate procedures for encouraging social help and building solid associations with others. We will figure out how to develop sympathy and empathy towards ourselves as well as other people, and to rest on our encouraging groups of people in the midst of hardship.

So let us embrace the force of social help with open hearts and receptive outlooks, realizing that it is through the strength of our connections that we can genuinely flourish notwithstanding affliction. Allow us to sustain our associations with others and deal backing to people around us, knowing that together, we are more grounded.

Chapter 7: Embracing Authenticity

Grasping Credibility

Validness is something beyond a popular expression; an essential part of carrying on with a life is consistent with ourselves. Yet, what's the significance here to be bona fide, and for what reason is it so significant? At its center, realness is tied in with living in arrangement with our qualities, convictions, and wants, as opposed to adjusting to the assumptions or norms of others.

At the point when we are real, we appear as our actual selves, without misrepresentation or façade. We talk and act from the heart, offering our viewpoints, sentiments, and feelings with trustworthiness and uprightness. Credibility expects us to be defenseless, to embrace our defects and weaknesses, and to appear really in our connections and collaborations with others.

Living genuinely is generally difficult, particularly in a world that frequently esteems similarity and fitting in over distinction and uniqueness. We might fear judgment or dismissal if we really think it wise to act naturally, driving us to take cover behind veils of flawlessness or similarity. Nonetheless, the cost of similarity is steep, denying us of the valuable chance to carry on with a day to day existence that is consistent with ourselves and keeping the world the gift from getting our genuine selves.

Additionally, legitimacy is fundamental for our own prosperity and satisfaction. At the point when we live really, we experience a feeling of compatibility and arrangement inside ourselves, permitting us to live with more prominent harmony, happiness, and satisfaction. Legitimacy additionally encourages further and more significant associations with others, as we can appear genuinely in our connections, permitting others to do likewise.

In the parts that follow, we will investigate systems for embracing legitimacy and carrying on with a daily existence lined up with our actual selves. We will figure out how to defeat the apprehension about judgment, develop self-acknowledgment, and live in arrangement with our qualities and convictions. So let us embrace the force of validness with open hearts and receptive outlooks, realizing that it is through being consistent with ourselves that we can genuinely flourish and carry on with an existence of significance and reason.

Defeating the Feeling of dread toward Judgment

One of the greatest obstructions to living legitimately is the apprehension about judgment from others. We stress over what others will think or say if we truly feel compelled to act naturally, driving us to take cover behind veils of congruity and flawlessness. Be that as it may, actually, the anxiety toward judgment is much of the time more weakening than the actual judgment.

Conquering the feeling of dread toward judgment is tied in with perceiving that others' assessments of us are not an impression of our value or worth. It's tied in with figuring out how to isolate our healthy identity worth from the decisions and assessments of others, realizing that our value is innate and not reliant upon outer approval.

One strong procedure for defeating the apprehension about judgment is to develop self-empathy and self-acknowledgment. At the point when we figure out how to acknowledge ourselves precisely as we are, defects and all, we become less dependent on outside approval and more sure about our own value. We perceive that we genuinely deserve love and acknowledgment, paying little mind to what others might think or say.

One more procedure for defeating the apprehension about judgment is to challenge our convictions and suspicions about judgment. Frequently, our anxiety toward judgment depends on silly convictions or misshaped thinking designs. By testing these convictions and supplanting them with more reasonable and enabling convictions, we can liberate ourselves from the grasp of dread and live more really.

Additionally, it's memorable's fundamental that not every person will pass judgment or condemn us for acting naturally. As a matter of fact, many individuals will respect and regard us for daring to appear legitimately in a world that frequently esteems congruity over uniqueness. By encircling ourselves with strong and tolerating individuals, we can make a place of refuge to communicate our thoughts unafraid of judgment.

In the sections that follow, we will investigate systems for beating the anxiety toward judgment and embracing our legitimate selves with boldness and certainty. We will figure out how to develop self-empathy and self-acknowledgment, challenge our convictions about judgment, and encircle ourselves with steady and tolerating individuals who commend our validness.

So let us embrace the excursion of defeating the anxiety toward judgment with open hearts and receptive outlooks, realizing that it is through thinking for even a second to act naturally that we can genuinely flourish and carry on with an existence of validness and reason.

Developing Self-Acknowledgment

Key to living legitimately is the act of self-acknowledgment — a profound and unqualified hug of ourselves, including our assets, shortcomings, and blemishes. Developing self-acknowledgment includes recognizing and embracing all parts of what our identity is, without judgment or analysis.

Frequently, we are our own cruelest pundits, holding ourselves to outlandishly exclusive expectations and censuring ourselves for missing the mark. However, genuine self-acknowledgment expects us to relinquish the requirement for flawlessness and embrace ourselves with consideration and empathy, similarly as we would a dear companion.

One strong procedure for developing self-acknowledgment is to rehearse self-empathy. At the point when we treat ourselves with the very warmth and understanding that we would propose to a companion in the midst of hardship, we establish a sustaining and strong internal climate where self-acknowledgment can thrive.

One more key part of developing self-acknowledgment is to challenge the internal pundit — the voice in our minds that lets us know we're not adequate or deserving of affection and acknowledgment. By perceiving that the internal pundit isn't the reality of what our identity is nevertheless just a result of our molding and previous encounters, we can start to relax its hold and develop a more empathetic and tolerating relationship with ourselves.

In addition, developing self-acknowledgment includes embracing our defects as a fundamental piece of what makes us human. Rather than endeavoring to stow away or fix our imperfections, we can figure out how to celebrate them as novel parts of our distinction and humankind.

In the parts that follow, we will investigate techniques for developing self-acknowledgment and embracing ourselves with graciousness and empathy. We will figure out how to challenge the inward pundit, practice self-sympathy, and praise our blemishes as a fundamental piece of what our identity is.

So let us embrace the act of developing self-acknowledgment with open hearts and receptive outlooks, realizing that it is through embracing ourselves precisely as we are that we can genuinely flourish and carry on with an existence of legitimacy and satisfaction.

Living in Arrangement

Living legitimately expects us to adjust our contemplations, activities, and values with our actual selves. At the point when we live in arrangement, we experience a profound feeling of harmoniousness and honesty, permitting us to live with more noteworthy reason and satisfaction.

Living in arrangement includes being consistent with ourselves in all parts of our lives — our connections, professions, leisure activities, and special goals. It implies paying attention to our inward insight and instinct and respecting our most profound longings and goals, regardless of whether they separate from cultural standards or assumptions.

One lifestyle choice in arrangement is to distinguish our basic beliefs — the core values that characterize what our identity and makes the biggest difference to us. At the point when we live in arrangement with our qualities, we decide and choices that are reliable with our actual selves, prompting more prominent genuineness and satisfaction.

Also, living in arrangement expects us to rehearse genuineness in our associations with others. It implies appearing genuinely in our associations, talking our reality with trustworthiness and respectability, and regarding the reality of others without judgment or analysis.

Living in arrangement is a continuous work on, requiring care, mindfulness, and mental fortitude. It includes ceaselessly checking in with ourselves to guarantee that our considerations, activities, and values are lined up with our actual selves, and making changes on a case by case basis to remain consistent with what our identity is.

In the sections that follow, we will investigate rehearses for living in arrangement and adjusting our contemplations, activities, and values with our actual selves. We will figure out how to stand by listening to our internal insight, distinguish our guiding principle, and practice credibility in our connections and collaborations with others.

So let us embrace the act of living in arrangement with open hearts and receptive outlooks, realizing that it is through conforming to our actual selves that we can genuinely flourish and carry on with an existence of validness and reason.

Chapter 8: The Courage to Create

Embracing Innovativeness

Imagination isn't held for craftsmen and performers; it is a key part of the human experience, fundamental for development, self-articulation, and self-improvement. Embracing imagination includes perceiving the intrinsic inventive potential inside every one of us and sustaining it as a significant asset for exploring life's difficulties and valuable open doors.

Innovativeness is about something beyond creating show-stoppers or music; it's tied in with moving toward existence with interest, creative mind, and a receptiveness to additional opportunities. It's tied in with seeing the world with a new perspective and tracking down imaginative answers for issues of all shapes and sizes.

Besides, imagination is an incredible asset for self-articulation and self-improvement. At the point when we participate in imaginative exercises, whether it's composition, painting, cooking, or cultivating, we tap into a profound well of motivation and self-disclosure, permitting us to communicate our thoughts legitimately and investigate new parts of our personality.

In any case, embracing imagination is generally difficult, particularly in a world that frequently esteems efficiency and effectiveness over creative mind and investigation. We might fear judgment or analysis if we feel compelled to articulate our thoughts innovatively, driving us to stifle our imaginative motivations and adjust to cultural assumptions.

In any case, the advantages of embracing imagination far offset the dangers. Imagination has been connected to various advantages, including further developed critical thinking abilities, improved close to home prosperity, and expanded flexibility notwithstanding difficulty.

In the sections that follow, we will investigate systems for embracing imagination and taking advantage of our natural innovative potential. We will figure out how to beat normal snags to imagination, develop a mentality of interest and liberality, and support our innovative soul through standard practice and self-articulation.

So let us embrace the force of imagination with open hearts and receptive outlooks, realizing that it is through embracing our innovative potential that we can genuinely flourish and carry on with an existence of significance and satisfaction.

Conquering Imaginative Blocks

Notwithstanding its significance, inventiveness is much of the time thwarted by different hindrances that can block our capacity to completely articulate our thoughts. These hindrances, known as imaginative blocks, can appear in many structures, like apprehension, self-uncertainty, hairsplitting, and absence of motivation.

Beating innovative blocks expects us to defy these snags head-on and foster systems for exploring them really. One normal impediment to innovativeness is dread — the apprehension about disappointment, of dismissal, or of not being sufficient. This dread can deaden us, keeping us from facing challenges and investigating groundbreaking thoughts.

Another normal obstruction is self-question — the internal voice that lets us know we're not adequately capable or innovative enough to create anything of significant worth. Self-uncertainty can sabotage our certainty and dissolve our confidence in our imaginative capacities, making it hard to pay attention to our gut feelings and face imaginative challenges.

Hairsplitting is one more typical obstruction to innovativeness, as it can lead us to set unthinkably exclusive requirements for us and become excessively reproachful of our work. At the point when we make progress toward flawlessness, we might turn out to be so centered around keeping away from botches that we neglect to face challenges or trial with groundbreaking thoughts, smothering our imagination simultaneously.

Absence of motivation is one more deterrent to imagination, as it can leave us feeling stuck and deadened. While we're battling to find motivation, it's not difficult to become deterred and abandon our inventive interests through and through.

In any case, conquering imaginative blocks is conceivable with the right techniques and outlook. One successful technique is to rehearse self-empathy and self-acknowledgment, perceiving that inventive blocks are a characteristic piece of the innovative strategy and treating ourselves with graciousness and understanding when we experience them.

Another methodology is to develop a development outlook, embracing difficulties and misfortunes as any open doors for development and learning. At the point when we take on a development mentality, we become stronger notwithstanding innovative blocks, realizing that each impediment is a potential chance to become more grounded and more imaginative.

In the sections that follow, we will investigate techniques for defeating imaginative blocks and releasing our full innovative potential. We will figure out how to stand up to our apprehensions and self-question, embrace blemish, and track down motivation in startling spots.

So let us embrace the test of conquering imaginative blocks with open hearts and receptive outlooks, realizing that it is through dealing with our deterrents directly that we can genuinely release our innovativeness and carry on with an existence of direction and satisfaction.

Developing an Inventive Mentality

Developing an imaginative mentality is fundamental for cultivating inventiveness in all everyday issues. It includes fostering an outlook of interest, trial and error, and liberality, permitting us to move toward difficulties and potential open doors with a new perspective and imaginative reasoning.

One critical part of developing an innovative mentality is to embrace interest — the eagerness to clarify some things, investigate groundbreaking thoughts, and search out original encounters. At the point when we approach existence with interest, we become more open to additional opportunities and more ready to face challenges and trial with various methodologies.

One more significant part of developing an inventive outlook is to rehearse trial and error — the eagerness to attempt new things, commit errors, and gain from disappointment. At the point when we embrace trial and error, we become stronger notwithstanding difficulties, realizing that each disappointment is a chance to learn and develop.

Besides, developing an innovative mentality includes fostering a disposition of liberality — the readiness to think about new points of view, challenge our suspicions, and embrace equivocalness. At the point when we approach issues with a receptive outlook, we become more open to novel thoughts and more imaginative in our critical thinking.

Yet, developing an imaginative outlook is generally difficult, particularly in a world that frequently esteems sureness and congruity over investigation and development. We might be adapted to search out the "right" reply or the "protected" way, driving us to smother our imagination and adjust to laid out standards.

Be that as it may, the advantages of developing an innovative mentality are significant. Imagination has been connected to various advantages, including further developed critical thinking abilities, improved close to home prosperity, and expanded versatility despite misfortune.

In the parts that follow, we will investigate methodologies for developing an imaginative outlook and releasing our full innovative potential. We will figure out how to embrace interest, trial and error, and liberality, permitting us to move toward existence with imagination and development.

So let us embrace the act of developing an innovative outlook with open hearts and receptive outlooks, realizing that it is through embracing our intrinsic inventiveness that we can genuinely flourish and carry on with an existence of direction and satisfaction.

Supporting the Inventive Soul

Supporting the inventive soul is fundamental for keeping an energetic and prospering innovative practice. It includes making opportunity for imaginative pursuits, looking for motivation from different sources, and embracing disappointment as a characteristic piece of the inventive flow.

One significant part of sustaining the imaginative soul is to focus on imagination in our regular routines. This implies cutting out time for imaginative exercises, whether it's composition, painting, cooking, or planting, and regarding these exercises as holy ceremonies that support our spirits and feed our inventiveness.

Looking for motivation from assorted sources is one more pivotal part of sustaining the innovative soul. Motivation can emerge out of many spots — craftsmanship, nature, writing, music, or even regular encounters — and presenting ourselves to a large number of impacts can start novel thoughts and light our imaginative interests.

Besides, embracing disappointment as a characteristic piece of the inventive strategy is fundamental for sustaining the innovative soul. Innovativeness isn't tied in with abstaining from botches or creating amazing work; it's tied in with facing challenges, exploring different avenues regarding novel thoughts, and gaining from disappointment. At the point when we embrace disappointment as a necessary piece of the imaginative excursion, we become stronger even with misfortunes and more able to face inventive challenges.

Yet, sustaining the imaginative soul isn't just about individual practice; it's likewise about developing a steady and supporting inventive local area. Encircling ourselves with other inventive people who share our interests and comprehend the difficulties of the innovative strategy can offer significant help and consolation, assisting us with remaining propelled and roused on our imaginative excursion.

In the sections that follow, we will investigate techniques for supporting the imaginative soul and developing an energetic and prospering inventive practice. We will figure out how to focus on imagination in our day to day routines, look for motivation from different sources, embrace disappointment as a characteristic piece of the innovative flow, and develop a strong and supporting inventive local area.

So let us embrace the act of supporting the imaginative soul with open hearts and receptive outlooks, realizing that it is through sustaining our innovative interests that we can genuinely flourish and carry on with an existence of direction and satisfaction.

Chapter 9: Embracing Change

Figuring out the Idea of Progress

Change is an unavoidable and steady part of life, winding around its way through the texture of our reality with unflinching industriousness. However, notwithstanding its certainty, change frequently brings out sensations of vulnerability, dread, and opposition. Understanding the idea of progress is the most vital move toward embracing it with transparency and acknowledgment.

Change takes many structures, from the unpretentious movements that happen inside us as we develop and advance, to the seismic changes that reshape our general surroundings. It can appear as changes in our connections, our professions, our wellbeing, or our conditions, provoking us to adjust and develop accordingly.

Besides, change is an impetus for self-improvement and change. It pushes us out of our usual ranges of familiarity, constraining us to stand up to our feelings of dread, beat snags, and find new parts of ourselves. While change can be awkward and problematic, it additionally holds the commitment of development, recharging, and self-disclosure.

In any case, in spite of its extraordinary potential, change is frequently met with obstruction. We stick to natural examples and schedules, dreading the obscure and the vulnerability that change brings. We might oppose change out of dread of disappointment, apprehension about misfortune, or anxiety toward the obscure, sticking to the well-being and security of the natural.

Notwithstanding, opposing change just draws out our torment and keeps us from completely embracing the amazing open doors for development and change that change offers. Rather than opposing change, we can decide to embrace it with transparency and acknowledgment, confiding during the time spent life and the insight of the universe.

In the sections that follow, we will investigate techniques for embracing change and exploring life's advances with flexibility and effortlessness. We will figure out how to develop versatility, embrace vulnerability, and consider change to be a chance for development and self-disclosure.

So let us embrace the certainty of progress with open hearts and receptive outlooks, realizing that it is through embracing change that we can genuinely develop, advance, and flourish.

Exploring Changes

Life is a progression of changes — snapshots of progress that mark the section starting with one part of our lives then onto the next. These advances can take many structures, from significant life altering situations, for example, profession changes, relationship movements, or migration, to additional unobtrusive changes in our points of view, needs, or characters. Exploring changes requires flexibility, versatility, and an eagerness to embrace the vulnerability and obscure that accompanies change.

One critical part of exploring changes is perceiving that they are a characteristic piece of the human experience. Advances are not irregularities to be stayed away from or dreaded yet rather potential open doors for development, reestablishment, and self-revelation. By reexamining changes as any open doors for development, we can move toward them with transparency and interest, confiding in our capacity to explore the unexplored world.

One more significant part of exploring advances is creating versatility — the capacity to return quickly from misfortunes, adjust to new conditions, and flourish notwithstanding change. Versatility isn't tied in with keeping away from difficulties or difficulties yet rather turning around them head-on, with boldness and assurance, and arising more grounded and savvier on the opposite side.

Additionally, exploring changes expects us to develop mindfulness and self-sympathy — to perceive and respect our feelings, needs, and wants as we explore the high points and low points of life. By rehearsing mindfulness and self-empathy, we can explore changes effortlessly and beauty, realizing that we have the internal assets to endure any hardship.

However, exploring advances is generally difficult, particularly when confronted with vulnerability, dread, or obstruction. We might feel overpowered by the progressions occurring around us, uncertain of how to push ahead or where to go for help. At these times, it's fundamental for rest on our encouraging groups of people — to contact companions, family, or tutors for direction and consolation.

In the sections that follow, we will investigate systems for exploring advances and embracing the open doors for development and self-disclosure that change brings. We will figure out how to develop flexibility, mindfulness, and self-empathy, permitting us to explore life's changes with strength and effortlessness.

So let us embrace the excursion of exploring advances with open hearts and receptive outlooks, realizing that it is through embracing change that we can genuinely develop, advance, and flourish.

Developing Versatility

Even with change, flexibility is a strong partner. Developing versatility includes fostering the adaptability and flexibility to conform to new conditions and flourish in dubious times. It expects us to embrace the obscure with transparency and interest, as opposed to dread and opposition.

Versatility isn't tied in with having the option to foresee or control the future; it's tied in with having the option to answer successfully to anything life tosses our direction. It's tied in with developing an outlook of adaptability and genius, permitting us to explore change with elegance and strength.

One vital part of developing versatility is fostering a development outlook — the conviction that our capacities and knowledge can be created through exertion and experience. At the point when we approach existence with a development mentality, we consider difficulties to be open doors for development and learning, as opposed to dangers to our security or dependability.

One more significant part of developing versatility is rehearsing care — the capacity to remain present and mindful despite change, without becoming overpowered by dread or vulnerability. Care permits us to notice our considerations and feelings with separation, permitting us to answer change with clearness and poise.

Besides, developing flexibility includes fostering an eagerness to step beyond our usual ranges of familiarity and attempt new things. It implies embracing inconvenience as a characteristic piece of the development interaction and driving ourselves to extend our points of view and investigate additional opportunities.

In any case, developing versatility is generally difficult, particularly in a world that frequently esteems sureness and security over adaptability and strength. We might be enticed to grip to the security and security of the natural, opposing change out of dread of the unexplored world.

In the parts that follow, we will investigate systems for developing flexibility and flourishing in dubious times. We will figure out how to foster a development mentality, practice care, and embrace uneasiness as an impetus for development and change.

So let us embrace the act of developing versatility with open hearts and receptive outlooks, realizing that it is through embracing change that we can genuinely develop, advance, and flourish.

Embracing Change as an Open door

Change is in many cases seen from the perspective of misfortune and disturbance, yet it additionally presents a chance for development, learning, and self-disclosure. Embracing change as an open door expects us to reexamine our viewpoint, moving from an outlook of dread and protection from one of receptiveness and plausibility.

One vital part of embracing change as an open door is perceiving the potential for development and change that exists in each change. Indeed, even the most troublesome and testing changes can be impetuses for self-improvement, offering us the valuable chance to master new abilities, foster flexibility, and develop a more profound comprehension of ourselves and our general surroundings.

One more significant part of embracing change as an open door is rehearsing appreciation — the capacity to find magnificence and gifts even amidst commotion and vulnerability. At the point when we approach significantly impact with a mentality of appreciation, we center around what we have instead of what we've lost, permitting us to see the silver linings and open doors for development that might have in any case slipped by everyone's notice.

In addition, embracing change as an open door includes relinquishing connections to the past and embracing the current second with transparency and acknowledgment. It implies confiding in the unfurling of life's excursion and embracing the obscure with boldness and interest, realizing that each change carries with it the chance for fresh starts and new points of view.

In any case, embracing change as an open door is generally difficult, particularly when confronted with startling or unwanted changes. We might feel overpowered by dread, despondency, or vulnerability, uncertain of how to push ahead or where to go for help. At these times, it's vital for rest on our encouraging groups of people — to connect with companions, family, or tutors for direction and support.

In the sections that follow, we will investigate techniques for embracing change as an open door and flourishing in the midst of vulnerability. We will figure out how to reevaluate our point of view, develop appreciation, and embrace the current second with transparency and acknowledgment, permitting us to explore life's progressions with flexibility and effortlessness.

So let us embrace the act of embracing change as an open door with open hearts and receptive outlooks, realizing that it is through embracing change that we can genuinely develop, advance, and flourish.

10

Chapter 10: Living Bravely Every Day

Embracing Mental fortitude

Mental fortitude isn't the shortfall of dread, yet the ability to act disregarding it. The internal strength empowers us to confront life's difficulties with versatility and assurance, in any event, when the way forward is dubious or overwhelming. Embracing mental fortitude expects us to step beyond our usual ranges of familiarity, to face our apprehensions head-on, and to make a striking move in quest for our objectives and dreams.

At its center, boldness is tied in with facing challenges and embracing weakness — the ability to put ourselves out there, in any event, when achievement isn't ensured. It's turning around our feelings of trepidation with trustworthiness and honesty, realizing that development and change frequently lie on the opposite side of dread.

Additionally, fortitude is a muscle that can be fortified with training. Each time we overcome our feelings of dread and make an unequivocal move, we construct our mental fortitude muscles, turning out to be stronger and enabled even with life's difficulties.

Yet, embracing fortitude is generally difficult, particularly when confronted with vulnerability or misfortune. We might feel deadened by dread, self-uncertainty, or frailty, uncertain of whether we have the stuff to defeat the hindrances in our way.

At these times, it's memorable's fundamental that mental fortitude isn't tied in with being bold, yet about being willing to act notwithstanding our feelings of dread. It's tied in with perceiving that we are prepared to do more than we suspect, and that development and change frequently expect us to step beyond our usual ranges of familiarity and embrace the unexplored world.

In the sections that follow, we will investigate techniques for embracing boldness and confronting life's difficulties with strength and assurance. We will figure out how to stand up to our feelings of trepidation, make an intense move, and develop the inward solidarity to beat anything that deterrents might come our direction.

So let us embrace the act of embracing fortitude with open hearts and receptive outlooks, realizing that it is through embracing our feelings of trepidation that we can genuinely develop, advance, and flourish.

Rehearsing Weakness

Weakness is in many cases misjudged as a shortcoming, however as a general rule, it is a wellspring of solidarity and validness in our connections and collaborations with others. Rehearsing weakness expects us to embrace our blemishes and show up truly, in any event, when it feels awkward or hazardous.

At its center, weakness is tied in with being willing to allow others to see us as we really are — to show our actual selves, imperfections and all, without misrepresentation or veneer. It's tied in with freeing ourselves up to the chance of dismissal or judgment, realizing that genuine association and closeness expect us to be recognized the truth about and acknowledged.

Rehearsing weakness isn't tied in with oversharing or revealing our most profound mysteries to everybody we meet. It's tied in with being willing to share our contemplations, sentiments, and encounters legitimately and transparently with those we trust, realizing that weakness is the way to building further and more significant associations.

Besides, rehearsing weakness expects us to develop self-empathy and self-acknowledgment — to treat ourselves with graciousness and understanding, in any event, when we feel uncovered or powerless. At the point when we practice self-sympathy, we become less dependent on outside approval and more positive about our own value, permitting us to appear truly in our associations with others.

However, rehearsing weakness is generally difficult, particularly in a world that frequently esteems strength and emotionlessness over weakness and realness. We might fear dismissal or judgment if we think it wise to act naturally, driving us to take cover behind veils of flawlessness or congruity.

At these times, it's memorable's fundamental that weakness is definitely not an indication of shortcoming, however an indication of mental fortitude and strength. It's tied in with daring to be blemished, to embrace our weaknesses, and to appear legitimately in our connections and collaborations with others.

In the sections that follow, we will investigate techniques for rehearsing weakness and embracing validness in our connections and communications with others. We will figure out how to develop self-empathy, fabricate trust and closeness, and make further associations with everyone around us.

So let us embrace the act of rehearsing weakness with open hearts and receptive outlooks, realizing that it is through embracing our weaknesses that we can genuinely interface with others and carry on with an existence of credibility and satisfaction.

Making A strong Move

Making a strong move is a foundation of living courageously consistently. It expects us to step beyond our usual ranges of familiarity, to face challenges, and to seek after our objectives and dreams earnestly and conviction, even notwithstanding vulnerability or dread.

At its center, making a strong move is tied in with daring to depend on our instincts and seek after our interests, in any event, when the way forward is muddled or full of obstructions. It's tied in with embracing the obscure with transparency and interest, confiding in our capacities and instinct to direct us forward.

Making a striking move frequently expects us to face our feelings of trepidation and instabilities — to push past the questions and self-restricting convictions that keep us away from chasing after our fantasies. It's tied in with perceiving that disappointment isn't the stopping point, yet just a venturing stone on the way to progress.

In addition, making a strong move includes putting forth clear expectations and objectives, and afterward finding a way definitive ways to carry them to completion. It's tied in with assuming a sense of ownership with our own lives and decisions, and declining to be kept down by dread or self-question.

However, making a striking move is generally difficult, particularly when confronted with vulnerability or opposition. We might feel incapacitated by dread of disappointment, or overpowered by the tremendousness of the assignment ahead. At these times, it's memorable's fundamental that fortitude isn't the shortfall of dread, however the eagerness to act regardless of it.

In the parts that follow, we will investigate procedures for making a strong move and chasing after our objectives and dreams with boldness and assurance. We will figure out how to go up against our feelings of dread, set clear aims, and move toward making the existence we want.

So let us embrace the act of making an intense move with open hearts and receptive outlooks, realizing that it is through facing challenges and chasing after our interests that we can genuinely live courageously consistently.

Developing Versatility

Versatility is the capacity to return from misfortunes and difficulty with elegance and constancy. It's turning around life's difficulties with mental fortitude and flexibility, and tracking down strength despite misfortune.

At its center, flexibility is a mentality — an approach to moving toward life's highs and lows with positive thinking, assurance, and self-conviction. It's tied in with perceiving that misfortunes are a characteristic piece of the human experience, and that we have the inward assets to conquer them.

Developing versatility expects us to foster survival techniques and emotionally supportive networks that assist us with exploring life's difficulties with beauty and flexibility. It includes rehearsing taking care of oneself and self-sympathy, and contacting others for help and support when we really want it most.

Also, developing versatility includes rethinking our viewpoint on disappointment and affliction — to see them not as indications of shortcoming, but rather as any open doors for development and learning. At the point when we embrace disappointment as a characteristic piece of the development cycle, we become stronger despite misfortunes, realizing that each disappointment is a chance to learn and develop.

Yet, developing strength is generally difficult, particularly when confronted with critical difficulties or affliction. We might feel overpowered by dread, uncertainty, or gloom, uncertain of how to push ahead or where to go for help.

At these times, it's fundamental for rest on our encouraging groups of people — to connect with companions, family, or tutors for direction and consolation. By developing versatility, we can face life's hardships with effortlessness and steadiness, realizing that we have the internal strength and flexibility to conquer anything difficulties might come our direction.

In the parts that follow, we will investigate procedures for developing versatility and returning from mishaps with elegance and determination. We will figure out how to embrace disappointment as a characteristic piece of the development interaction, and to consider difficulties to be open doors for development and self-revelation.

So let us embrace the act of developing flexibility with open hearts and receptive outlooks, realizing that it is through versatility that we can genuinely flourish and live courageously consistently.

Conclusion:

Reflection on Mental fortitude

As we reach the finish of this excursion, it's vital for pause for a minute to consider the extraordinary force of boldness. All through this book, we've investigated the idea of fortitude — the ability to confront life's difficulties with flexibility and assurance. We've perceived how boldness isn't the shortfall of dread, yet the eagerness to act notwithstanding it. It's tied in with venturing beyond our usual ranges of familiarity, embracing weakness, and making a strong move in quest for our objectives and dreams.

Pondering our excursion of embracing fortitude, we can perceive how it has molded and changed us. We've overcome our apprehensions, stood up to our questions, and moved toward making the lives we want. We've discovered that boldness isn't something we're brought into the world with, however something we develop through training and diligence. A muscle develops further with each challenge we face, each dread we vanquish, and every strong move we make.

In addition, pondering mental fortitude helps us to remember the endless snapshots of courage and flexibility we've seen in ourselves as well as other people. From little demonstrations of boldness, such as supporting ourselves or taking a stab at a new thing, to bigger demonstrations of mental fortitude, such as confronting significant life advances or chasing after our fantasies despite everything, we've perceived how boldness has the ability to change lives and impact the world.

However, our excursion of embracing fortitude is not even close to finished. As we push ahead, let us convey the illustrations we've learned with us — the significance of overcoming our apprehensions, embracing weakness, and making a strong move in quest for our fantasies. Allow us to keep on developing mental fortitude in our lives, realizing that it is through embracing our feelings of trepidation that we can genuinely develop, advance, and flourish.

So let us pause for a minute to consider the boldness we've developed and the changes it has brought into our lives. Allow us to praise our strength, our assurance, and our readiness to embrace the obscure with open hearts and receptive outlooks. Also, let us convey the soul of boldness with us as we proceed with our process forward, knowing that with fortitude close by, there is no test we can't survive.

Appreciation for Weakness

As we finish up our investigation of dauntlessness, it's essential to offer thanks for the strength and genuineness that weakness brings to our lives. All through this excursion, we've dug into the idea of weakness — the readiness to show up genuinely, defects and all, and to allow ourselves to be seen and known by others.

Appreciation for weakness helps us to remember the force of legitimacy in encouraging profound and significant associations with others. It's through weakness that we develop closeness, trust, and sympathy in our connections, permitting us to fashion certifiable associations in light of genuineness and common regard.

Additionally, offering thanks for weakness helps us to remember the boldness it takes to be powerless — to gamble with dismissal or judgment to show our actual selves to the world. A bold demonstration expects us to defy our feelings of trepidation and weaknesses, and to embrace our flaws with effortlessness and acknowledgment.

However, weakness isn't just about showing our shortcomings; it's likewise about embracing our assets and commending our uniqueness. It's tied in with possessing our accounts, embracing our validness, and standing tall despite difficulty.

As we offer thanks for weakness, let us additionally stretch out appreciation to ourselves for daring to be defenseless — to show up really, to talk our reality, and to allow ourselves to be seen and known by others. Allow us to respect the strength and versatility it takes to embrace weakness, realizing that it is through weakness that we develop further associations, more extravagant encounters, and more prominent satisfaction in our lives.

So let us pause for a minute to offer thanks for the strength and validness that weakness brings to our lives. Allow us to commend the mental fortitude it takes to be defenseless, and the profound associations it encourages with others. Also, let us convey the soul of weakness with us as we proceed with our process forward, knowing that with weakness close by, there is no restriction to the profundity of association and satisfaction we can insight in our lives.

Obligation to Activity

As we finish up our investigation of living valiantly consistently, now is the right time to promise to keep making a striking move and seeking after our objectives and dreams earnestly and conviction. All through this excursion, we've found the groundbreaking force of fortitude — the ability to deal with life's difficulties directly and to move toward making the lives we want.

Resolving to activity implies defining clear expectations and objectives for ourselves, and afterward finding a way purposeful ways to carry them to completion. It's tied in with perceiving our value and deservingness of the existence we want, and declining to agree to anything short of our most genuine, most valid selves.

In addition, resolving to activity implies embracing the obscure with transparency and interest, and confiding in our capacities and instinct to direct us forward. It's tied in with venturing beyond our usual ranges of familiarity, facing challenges, and seeking after our interests with enduring assurance, even despite vulnerability or dread.

In any case, resolving to activity isn't just about defining objectives and doing whatever it may take to accomplish them; it's likewise about developing strength and constancy despite misfortunes and obstructions. It's tied in with perceiving that disappointment isn't the stopping point, yet just a venturing stone on the way to progress, and daring to get back up and attempt once more, regardless of how frequently we fall.

As we promise to activity, let us likewise focus on supporting and empowering ourselves en route. Allow us to rehearse self-sympathy and taking care of oneself, and commend our triumphs, regardless of how little. Allow us to advise ourselves that we are equipped for accomplishing anything we put our energy into, and that with boldness, assurance, and steadiness, there is no objective too huge or dream too overwhelming to even think about accomplishing.

So let us sincerely promise to activity, realizing that it is through making a strong move and seeking after our interests with relentless assurance that we can genuinely live courageously consistently. Allow us to embrace the obscure with fortitude and conviction, and confidence in our capacities to make the lives we want. Furthermore, let us convey the soul of responsibility with us as we proceed with our process forward, knowing that earnestly and steadiness close by, there isn't anything we can't accomplish.

Embracing Flexibility

In our last reflection on living fearlessly consistently, embracing flexibility as a core value in confronting misfortunes and difficulty with beauty and perseverance is fundamental. All through this excursion, we've experienced difficulties, hindrances, and snapshots of uncertainty, yet we've additionally found the inward strength and versatility to defeat them.

Embracing strength implies perceiving that misfortunes and disappointments are not the stopping point, but rather simply reroutes on the way to progress. It's tied in with returning quickly from affliction with effortlessness and assurance, and declining to allow difficulties to characterize us or keep us away from chasing after our fantasies.

Besides, embracing versatility implies developing an outlook of confidence and plausibility, even despite vulnerability or despondency. It's tied in with perceiving that each challenge presents a chance for development and learning, and that we have the internal assets to defeat anything that obstructions might come our direction.

In any case, embracing flexibility isn't just about enduring the hardships of life; it's additionally about tracking down strength and importance notwithstanding affliction. It's tied in with perceiving the silver linings and open doors for development that frequently go with troublesome times, and daring to embrace them with open hearts and receptive outlooks.

As we embrace versatility, let us likewise stretch out empathy and thoughtfulness to ourselves as well as other people. Allow us to recall that we are human, and that we as a whole face difficulties and misfortunes occasionally. Allow us to help and energize each other, and praise our flexibility and strength notwithstanding misfortune.

So let us embrace strength as a core value in our lives, realizing that it is through flexibility that we can genuinely flourish and live courageously consistently. Allow us to confront life's difficulties with beauty and assurance, and confidence in our capacities to beat anything impediments might come our direction. What's more, let us convey the soul of strength with us as we proceed with our process forward, knowing that with flexibility close by, there is no test too perfect to even consider surviving.

www.ingramcontent.com/pod-product-compliance
Lightning Source LLC
Chambersburg PA
CBHW031334130726

47988CB00007B/3119